Ancients in Their Own Words
Mesopotamians

Ancients in Their Own Words
Mesopotamians

MICHAEL KERRIGAN

Marshall Cavendish
Benchmark
New York

Other Marshall Cavendish Offices:
Marshall Cavendish International (Asia) Private Limited, 1 New Industrial Road, Singapore 536196 • Marshall Cavendish International (Thailand) Co Ltd. 253 Asoke, 12th Flr, Sukhumvit 21 Road, Klongtoey Nua, Wattana, Bangkok 10110, Thailand • Marshall Cavendish (Malaysia) Sdn Bhd, Times Subang, Lot 46, Subang Hi-Tech Industrial Park, Batu Tiga, 40000 Shah Alam, Selangor Darul Ehsan, Malaysia

Marshall Cavendish is a trademark of Times Publishing Limited

All websites were available and accurate when this book was sent to press.

Library of Congress Cataloging-in-Publication Data

Kerrigan, Michael, 1959–
Mesopotamians / by Michael Kerrigan.
p. cm. -- (Ancients in their own words)
Summary: "Offers insight into ancient times through the words of its peoples, featuring some of the most important written records from ancient Mesopotamia, including: the Sumerian King List, the Code of Hammurabi, the Hittite-Egyptian treaty of Kadesh, and the Epic of Gilgamesh, with examples of scripts carved into clay tablets and pillars using cuneiform letters"--Provided by publisher.
Includes bibliographical references and index.

ISBN 978-1-60870-066-0

1. Iraq--Civilization--To 634--Juvenile literature. 2. Quotations--Translations into English--Juvenile literature. I. Title.

DS71.K416 2010
935--dc22

2009033476

Editorial and design by
Amber Books Ltd
Bradley's Close
74–77 White Lion Street
London N1 9PF
United Kingdom
www.amberbooks.co.uk

Project Editor: Michael Spilling
Design: Joe Conneally
Picture research: Natascha Spargo

For Marshall Cavendish Corporation:
Editor: Deborah Grahame
Publisher: Michelle Bisson
Art Director: Anahid Hamparian

CONTENTS

INTRODUCTION

THE EARLIEST HUMANS LIVED FOR THOUSANDS OF YEARS AS HUNTER-GATHERERS—hunting animals and gathering fruit, nuts, leaves, and other foods. Such a lifestyle is fine, but can only sustain small communities. People in these communities generally have to live as nomads—always on the move.

About 10,000 years ago, however, people figured out that they could cut back on the gathering and traveling part of their lifestyle. By scattering seeds they had picked, they could grow their own food, especially grains. One of the first regions in which this great revolution took place appears to have been the "Fertile Crescent," the name for a crescent-shaped area of land in the Middle East stretching up through what is now Iraq and across into Syria. The Tigris and Euphrates rivers run along the length of the Fertile Crescent from north to south. The Greeks called this country Mesopotamia, meaning "between the rivers."

By planting crops, the peoples here were able to produce enough food to live on without having to keep moving around. They could construct permanent buildings, establish settlements, and build cities. Because they could grow more than enough food to survive on, they used the surplus for trading purposes. There was a surplus of people too, and some could be spared to work as craftspeople and artisans, rather than toiling in the fields.

Power, Wealth, and Writing

Some people became soldiers because, at this time, wealthy and powerful individuals were taking charge as kings. Increasingly they were going to war with one another. Civilization was not necessarily what we today would call "civilized." As powerful states took form—first in Sumeria, to the south, and then in Akkad and Assyria, farther to the north—their governments supported themselves by taxing their people and taking tribute from those they conquered. To keep track of these payments, and of trade in general, they developed written scripts that were "written" by making marks in wet clay with a sharpened stick. The characters they produced in this way have a distinctive wedge-shape, and so are known as "cuneiform" from the Latin word *cuneus*, meaning "wedge."

◀ The cradle of Mesopotamian civilization, the Euphrates River flows from eastern Turkey in the north down to the Gulf of Arabia at the southernmost point of modern-day Iraq.

THE SARGON LEGEND

"SARGON THE GREAT" DESERVED HIS TITLE: THE FOUNDER OF MESOPOTAMIA'S FIRST EMPIRE WAS CERTAINLY AN IMPORTANT RULER, BUT HE WAS AN EVEN GREATER MYTHMAKER.

Sargon the Great (reigned 2270 to 2215 BCE) appeared out of nowhere in the twenty-fourth century BCE, when he suddenly seized power in the city-state of Kish. It is thought he had served as an official before he overthrew King Ur-Zababa in a rebellion. His real name is as mysterious as his origins. He gave himself the title Sharru-ken, or Sargon, which means, "Lawful King," perhaps because he was aware that he was not exactly lawful.

Beloved of Inana

In fact, the "Legend of Sargon," which he himself encouraged, makes no secret of his humble origins. Some stories describe how he was found floating in a basket on a river, like Moses in the Bible. And the legend does not deny that Sargon seized the throne by violence.

It does, however, insist that Inana, the Sumerian goddess of love and war, helped him throughout. According to the legend, she advanced his career

◀ The Sumerian goddess Inana was known to the Babylonians and Assyrians as Ishtar. The Phoenicians worshiped her as Astarte. She was goddess of fertility, love, and war. To the Mesopotamians it made sense to have the same deity for love and war: both were seen as violent and destructive passions.

THE TRANSLATION

WHAT DOES IT MEAN?

The details may be colorful—even shocking—but the message of the inscription is very clear: Sargon's kingship was meant to be; it was the will of the goddess Inana.

❝ As evening fell one day, Sargon came to the royal palace with his regular deliveries. Ur-Zababa was sleeping in his sacred chamber. He had a dream... He made Sargon his cupbearer, giving him charge of drinks. Inana still stood by him.

Between five and ten days later, King Ur-Zababa ... was gripped by fear in his palace. Fluids rushed from his body, all down his own legs, and there was blood and pus mixed in. In his fear and distress, he was like a fish thrashing about in stagnant water.

Then the cupbearer Sargon had his own dream: he saw the goddess Inana drowning Ur-Zababa in a torrent of blood. As he slept, he moaned and chewed the earth. Hearing of his moaning, King Ur-Zababa had him summoned to his sacred presence and said: "Cupbearer, did you have a vision in the night?" Sargon replied: "My lord: here is the dream I had. I saw a young woman, standing to the heavens, her body as vast as the earth, as firm in her stance as the bottom of a wall. She drowned you in a terrible torrent, a river of blood—and for my sake." **❞**

▶ Akkadian cuneiform is very concise, which means that a lengthy text can be expressed in just a few lines. The first Mesopotamian scripts are believed to have been developed for keeping records of such things as tax payments, trading transactions, and stored supplies.

and protected him. When Ur-Zababa became aware of Sargon's ambition and sent him off with a message containing secret instructions to have Sargon killed, Inana intervened to save him.

The Empire of Akkad

Sargon achieved a great deal as king. Having made himself the king of Kish, around 2234 BCE, he built an empire in the northern part of Mesopotamia (in modern-day Iraq). He began by invading the neighboring kingdom of Uruk, and then went to war against the other cities of Sumer before crossing the Tigris and Euphrates rivers to take territories in

Elam, to the east, and Syria, to the west. He established a capital at Agade, and it was for this reason that his empire became known as "Akkad." Large and powerful though it was, this empire quickly fell apart after its founder died, but its splendors were remembered in the region for centuries after. So was the Akkadian language, which was spoken in the region for the next 2,000 years.

The memory of Sargon was so glorious that when, a thousand years later, another official seized power in Assyria and wanted a way of making his rule look lawful, he took on the title of Sargon II. He knew that an aura of power surrounded this name.

▶ Sargon stands before the tree of life. Kings in Mesopotamia were seen not just as powerful men but as superhuman figures backed up by the gods.

▼ Kish (now Tell al-Uhaymir, in Iraq) was one of Sumer's oldest cities. Sargon the Great first came to power here.

AT THE GOD'S COMMAND

THIS INSCRIPTION, FROM THE AKKADIAN KINGDOM OF LAGASH, IS BEAUTIFULLY POETIC, BUT IT HAS A GREAT DEAL MORE TO SAY IF YOU READ BETWEEN THE LINES.

Piety, poetry, and political promotion come together in this inscription, believed to have been made in around the twenty-second century BCE. At that time, the city of Ngirsu was capital of the up-and-coming kingdom of Lagash. This state was establishing itself as the leading force in southern Sumerian affairs. A lengthy, powerfully poetic text was carved into two ceramic cylinders. The inscription was created when the clay was wet, then fired to hardness. Inscribed cylinders like this were often used in ancient Mesopotamia for recording dedications.

▼ You could hardly guess that this jumble of mud-brick ruins was the center of a prosperous and powerful state. The "Gudea Cylinders" serve to remind us of this great place.

THE TRANSLATION

WHAT DOES IT MEAN?
The inscription describes how King Gudea built the shrine to the god Ningursu on the deity's own orders. In the process, it makes clear that Gudea had the god's backing for his reign.

66 On a day when the destinies of heaven and earth were being laid down, Lagash lifted its head, so huge that it towered toward heaven...

Certainly, the heart of man overbrimmed its banks; certainly, the heart of the god Enlil overbrimmed its banks, pouring sweet water as the Tigris River.

In my dream, a lone man appeared, huge as the heavens, vast as earth. His head was like the head of a god; his arms were the wings of the Anzu bird, but his lower parts were the roaring floodwaters themselves. To his right and left, lions lay down. He gave me the command to build his temple, but I could not fully understand his plans. **99**

▶ Gudea died forty centuries ago, and his civilization disappeared not long afterward. Even so, this account of his divine destiny, carved into clay, can still be read.

The cylinders were placed in the foundations of new buildings as a permanent memorial. (Time has proved their makers right: long after their palaces and fortifications crumbled away to nothing, many of these inscribed cylinders have survived.)

A New Order

The inscription praises Ningursu, the Sumerian god of thunder and the protector of the state. It tells how King Gudea was inspired to build his temple here. The site was already sacred to Enlil, an even more sacred god associated with life, space, and air: Gudea set up his deity, Ningursu, as Enlil's son.

The inscription says that Ningursu's arms were the "wings of the Anzu bird." This monstrous, fire-breathing creature was a symbol of evil and destruction in Mesopotamian mythology. It was said to have stolen the foundation records of the universe from Enlil's temple, throwing the heavens and earth into total chaos and confusion.

Ningursu, though, caught and killed the Anzu bird and restored order once again. He took the

▶ This splendid statue of the twenty-second century BCE is of Gudea himself. It is made of calcite, which gives it a greenish tinge.

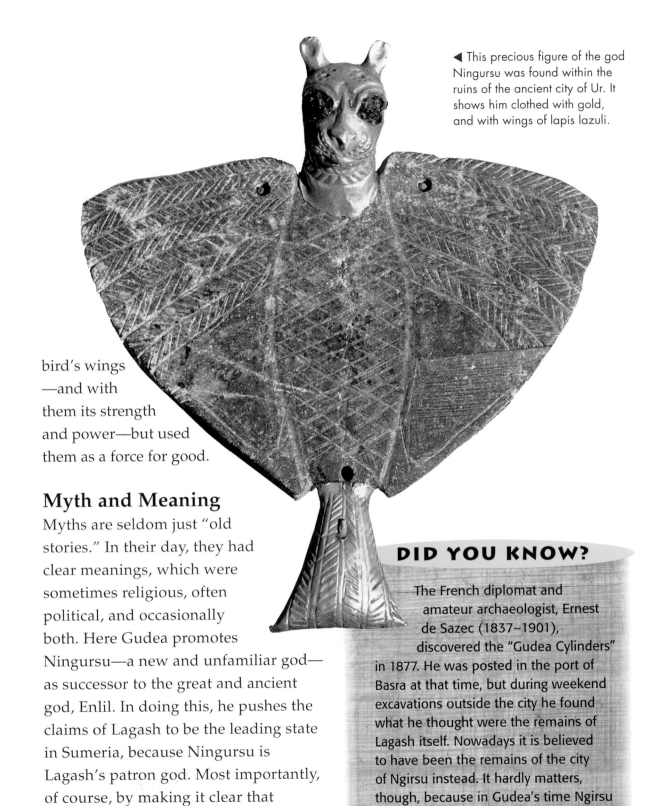

◀ This precious figure of the god Ningursu was found within the ruins of the ancient city of Ur. It shows him clothed with gold, and with wings of lapis lazuli.

bird's wings —and with them its strength and power—but used them as a force for good.

Myth and Meaning

Myths are seldom just "old stories." In their day, they had clear meanings, which were sometimes religious, often political, and occasionally both. Here Gudea promotes Ningursu—a new and unfamiliar god— as successor to the great and ancient god, Enlil. In doing this, he pushes the claims of Lagash to be the leading state in Sumeria, because Ningursu is Lagash's patron god. Most importantly, of course, by making it clear that Ningursu himself has given him his orders, Gudea is proclaiming his own greatness as Lagash's king.

DID YOU KNOW?

The French diplomat and amateur archaeologist, Ernest de Sazec (1837–1901), discovered the "Gudea Cylinders" in 1877. He was posted in the port of Basra at that time, but during weekend excavations outside the city he found what he thought were the remains of Lagash itself. Nowadays it is believed to have been the remains of the city of Ngirsu instead. It hardly matters, though, because in Gudea's time Ngirsu was probably the capital of the kingdom of Lagash.

MESOPOTAMIAN MEDICINE

A CLAY TABLET COVERED WITH CUNEIFORM TEXT TURNS OUT TO BE A MEDICAL MANUAL. AT FOUR THOUSAND YEARS OF AGE, IT IS PERHAPS THE EARLIEST EXAMPLE IN EXISTENCE.

Some time around 2100 BCE, an unknown scribe sat down and set to work recording a series of prescriptions for medical treatment. The inscriptions are too carefully done and too detailed to be dismissed only as notes. Was he writing a complete catalog of Mesopotamian medicine? The tablet we have provides fifteen separate "cures," but there may well have been a great many more. Some of the ingredients used, such as turtleshell, moonplant flower, and powdered willow bark, may seem exotic to us, but there are also very familiar ones like turpentine and thyme.

▼ The ancient city of Nippur in modern-day Iraq has been a treasure trove of tablets. These were inscribed with everything from scientific texts and mathematical tables, to temple records and schoolwork.

THE TRANSLATION

The inscriptions show what we might call superstition coming together with something more scientific to produce a surprisingly modern approach to medicine.

" Grind the bark of the pear tree up into a powder together with the flower of the moonplant. Pour on some wine, then stir in plain vegetable oil and add heated cedar oil.

Grind up seeds of the carpenter plant with Markazi resin and thyme. Stir the result into beer and then give it to a man to drink.

Add hot water to powdered, dried water snake and Amama-Shumkaspal plant, thorn roots, powdered Naga-plant, and powdered turpentine... Rub it into the affected area after it has been bathed. "

► Inscribed with care and clarity, apparently for ease of use, was this tablet created as part of a larger medical manual for a working doctor?

Powerful Prescriptions

To modern eyes, the treatments described here are an odd combination of mumbo-jumbo and genuine medicine. But by the standards of the time, the prescriptions seem strikingly modern. If we compare an Egyptian medical text of the time, we see that the pharaohs' doctors placed great reliance on incantations. The so-called "Metternich Stela," for example, is a large stone that is inscribed all over with what are clearly spells that the sufferer or the priest must recite to be cured.

The Egyptian priest might well have ground up this or that substance and mixed it with certain oils or wine as he uttered his prayers. But he would have done this to make an offering, not a medicine. He did it as part of his sacred ritual, a mark of devotion to the god to whom he was appealing for a cure. If, at the end of this ritual, the patient actually got better, it would have been taken for granted that this was the result of the god's intervention. By contrast, the Mesopotamian doctor obviously expects his or her prescription to work on its own, and there is no suggestion that any gods should be involved.

Ancient Aspirin

The fact that powdered willow bark was used is interesting. This substance contains salicylic acid, which is what makes modern aspirin work as a painkiller. Aspirin appears to have been widely known from prehistoric times, not just in Mesopotamia, but also in the New World.

◀ This figure, found amid the ruins of a Sumerian temple, seems to represent a priest or a scholar—or could it even be an ancient doctor?

18

Divine Doctoring

It would be wrong to assume that Mesopotamian medicine was entirely based on science, as we would understand it. We know from other inscriptions that healers who relied on rituals did exist, and that they appealed to the gods and sacred spirits for their cures.

And there may even have been a religious dimension to this more modern type of doctor. Was it just coincidence that this tablet was found at Nippur? This was one of Mesopotamia's oldest cities, dating from 5000 BCE or even earlier. It had established itself as the main shrine to Enlil, god of the universe. Even if the inscriptions on the tablet make no mention of Enlil, it may have been assumed that his assistance would be required.

▼ Ekur, the "House of the Mountain," above Nippur, was the main shrine of the god Enlil. Excavations are currently under way at what is believed to be its site.

A CATALOG OF KINGS

THE "SUMERIAN KING LIST" RECORDS THE REIGNS OF ANCIENT
SUMER'S EARLIEST RULERS. IT IS A STRANGE MIXTURE OF MYTH
AND HAZY HISTORY.

Books, as we know them today, were still many centuries away when the first civilizations rose and fell in Mesopotamia. Even paper was unknown, at least outside Egypt. Texts were written on tablets of wet clay. These had the advantage that they could be easily erased, though they could also be baked for permanence if required. More prestigious inscriptions were carved into ceramic cylinders, or prisms (a "prism" is any solid, multi-sided shape). What is known as the "Weld-Blundell Prism" is a good example.

THE TRANSLATION

WHAT DOES IT MEAN?

The Sumerian King List told its ancient readers that the kings of their own time came from a long and glorious line of rulers, who reigned for many lifetimes with the blessing of the gods.

66 The Office of King came down from heaven, landing at Eridu. At Eridu, Alulim was king. He reigned for 28,800 years. Alagar's reign lasted 36,000 years. Two kings. Between them they reigned for 64,800 years.

Eridu was conquered. Power passed to Badtibira. Enmenluanna ruled from Badtibira for 43,200 years. Enmengalanna ruled for 28,800 years. Dumuzisib ruled for 36,000 years. Three kings. They reigned for 108,000 years.

Badtibira was conquered. The place of kingship was set up at Larak. At Larak, Ensibzianna reigned for 28,800 years. One king. He ruled for 28,800 years. Larak was conquered. Power passed to Sippar. At Sippar Enmenduranna reigned as king for 21,000 years. One king. He reigned for 21,000 years. Sippar was conquered. The place of kingship was established at Shuruppak. At Shuruppak Ubardudu was king and reigned for 18,600 years. One king. He ruled for 18,600 years. Five cities. Eight kings. They ruled for 241,200 years. 99

◄ The Weld-Blundell Prism stands just 8 inches (20 cm) tall and 3.5 inches (9 cm) wide, but its inscription records the reigns of many kings.

Each of the prism's four faces has two columns of cuneiform text. This records the Sumerian rulers of the earliest age, the order of their succession, and the lengths of their reigns.

An Uncertain Situation

The prism was written around 1800 BCE in the city of Larsa on the Lower Euphrates River during a period of mounting instability in Sumer. Under Sargon the Great, Akkad, in central Mesopotamia, had been the dominant power. But Akkadian power had collapsed soon after Sargon died in 2215 BCE, allowing the southern city of Ur to increase its influence again.

King Ur-Nammu reigned from about 2112 to 2095 BCE. He worked with his son Shulgi to build an empire as great as Sargon's had been, but ruled from Ur. However, by the beginning of the second millennium BCE, Ur-Nammu's empire had also passed its height. A series of cities had then risen and fallen, taking their turns as imperial centers—Isin, Larsa, Manana, Kazullu, and finally Babylon had come to the fore, the greatest city the world had ever seen.

Chosen by the Gods

The problem for all these kings was that of proving their lawful right to rule. It did not seem enough simply to have come out on top in Sumer's seemingly never-ending struggle for power. Many of these kings must have been ambitious officials or soldiers who had seized the thrones of weaker men. But if they could establish their place in a lengthy succession of Sumerian kings dating back many thousands of years, their claims to supremacy would be confirmed.

The "King List" claimed reigns many lifetimes long for these glorious (and mostly mythical) predecessors, but as far as people in those times were concerned, it was the truth. To them it simply showed that these early monarchs must have had the blessing of the gods.

▼ The Weld-Blundell Prism was unearthed among these ruins at Babylon. Their inscribed records have by and large outlasted Mesopotamia's splendid cities.

▲ This is a boundary stone from Sippar, which, according to the "King List," was the center of power of King Enmenduranna for 21,000 years. This marker was placed much later, in the twelfth century BCE.

HAMMURABI'S CODE

IN THE EIGHTEENTH CENTURY BCE, A KING OF BABYLON HAD HIS LEGAL CODE CARVED INTO A SPLENDID BASALT PILLAR TO PROCLAIM THE POWER AND THE MAJESTY OF THE LAW.

Inscribed into a column of polished black basalt more than 7 feet (2.25 meters) tall, the Code of Hammurabi lists the laws of Babylon. More than this, though, its sheer magnificence makes us appreciate the dignity and the grandeur of the law. This must have been exactly what King Hammurabi had intended. Hammurabi was the sixth king of Babylon, ruling from about 1792 to 1750 BCE. Babylon was a relatively minor city when he came to the throne, but under his leadership it became the center of a mighty empire.

▼ The Akkadian cuneiform in which the code is written was in use across much of Mesopotamia in the eighteenth century BCE. Later, Babylon would develop its own script.

THE TRANSLATION

WHAT DOES IT MEAN?

A fair society, the Code of Hammurabi insisted, had to be shaped by a framework of god-given laws, rather than by the tyranny of the strong (even the king) over the weak.

" Whoever accuses someone of a crime in front of the elders, but fails to prove his claim is—if the charge is a capital one—to be put to death.

If he manages to prove his claim and gets the elders to impose a fine of grain or money, that fine is to go to him... Anyone who breaks into a house is to be executed at the spot where he made his entry and buried there.

Anyone who commits a robbery is to be executed. If the robber is not caught, then his victim will report the value of his loss under oath; the community shall then pay him compensation for what was taken.

If, when a house is on fire, one of those who has come to help put it out notices valuables in the house and takes them, he is to be thrown into that very fire...

If a group of conspirators meet in a tavern to plot a crime, and the tavern-keeper knows but does not report them, then she is as guilty as they are and shall be put to death... **"**

◀ The Code of Hammurabi proclaims not just the detailed rules but also the majesty of the law, given by the gods to ensure the smooth running of society.

▼ The excavated city of Susa. Susa is thought to have been founded around 4200 BCE and appears in Sumerian records from the twenty-first century BCE. It was conquered by Sargon the Great in 2330 BCE, but later gained independence as the Elamite capital.

In quick succession, Hammurabi conquered Isin, Larsa, Eshnunna, and Mari until he ruled most of central Mesopotamia. His successors were not as skilled in war or diplomacy as he had been, and so Babylon went into decline after Hammurabi's death.

Divine Justice

Hammurabi himself appears on the column. His picture can be found carved near to the top. We see him as a figure of immense, but not the ultimate, authority. Instead, we see him with his right arm raised in respect, as he is given the laws

of Babylon by the great sun god Shamash. The message is clear: the law is given to humanity by the gods. It is greater than any mortal, even a king, however powerful he may be.

The code is written in Akkadian cuneiform (the script that was used by the Babylonians in their early days). Altogether, it lists 282 laws. They cover everything from obvious crimes like robbery and theft to more complex questions of taxation, marriage and family relationships, and the regulations governing business deals and practice.

Presumed Innocent

In certain ways, Hammurabi's Code seems terrifying in its strictness: a great many relatively minor offenses are punishable by death. But it seems strikingly humane in other ways. In some respects, it even seems very modern.

For example, the code appears to accept that the individual accused of a crime should be assumed to be innocent by the court unless his or her accuser can prove their charge. And harsh penalties (including death) are in place for those making false accusations.

▶ Head of a Babylonian king, possibly Hammurabi, carved from diorite stone (1750 BCE). Critics have suggested that Hammurabi was chiefly concerned with safeguarding his own royal property, and goods and land he had confiscated from his enemies. But his code seems genuinely just and fair.

27

ALPHABETIC ORIGINS

UGARIT WAS A BUSY SEAPORT, TRADING EAST AND WEST BETWEEN
MESOPOTAMIA, THE MEDITERRANEAN, AND EGYPT. WAS IT HERE THAT
THE WORLD'S FIRST ALPHABET WAS WRITTEN?

Outside Ras Shamra, near Latakia, on Syria's Mediterranean coast, a peasant was plowing one day in 1928. When his plowshare got stuck he found that it had caught on the roof of an underground chamber, which turned out to be part of an ancient tomb. Archaeologists flocked to investigate. They found pottery and handcrafted items, as well as the remains of foundations and streets belonging to a city that had flourished eight thousand years ago.

A Trading Center

Ugarit had been a bustling port, with links across the ancient world. This was easy to tell from the things the archaeologists uncovered as they excavated. There were finds from down the coast in Egypt and across the sea in Cyprus and the Greek Islands, which were at this time going through their early Mycenaean phase. Traders from Ugarit had also ventured eastward, inland along the "Fertile Crescent" to the Tigris and Euphrates rivers. Between

those two rivers lay the land of Mesopotamia. It was from here that Ugarit's first cuneiform script had been brought. This skill of writing was perhaps Ugarit's most crucial import.

Cumbersome Cuneiform

The archaeologists discovered a fascinating fact. Even though Ugarit's people had started out writing in cuneiform, in the traditional Mesopotamian style, they had gradually changed the way they wrote. It is not hard to see why they would want to do this. Cuneiform was far too complicated for their needs. It was a "pictographic" form of writing, where each character was a sort of picture of what it represented.

THE INSCRIPTION

This tablet, found at Ugarit, dates from approximately 1400 BCE. It represents one of the first examples of alphabetical writing ever known.

WHAT DOES IT MEAN?
The "Ugarit Alphabet" has meaning far beyond anything that was actually written in it. The invention of the alphabet changed what writing was and what it could do.

There were more than five hundred different symbols, so mastering the skills of reading and writing pictographs might take a person many years.

This was fine in Mesopotamia, where there were armies of scribes available,

▲ Today, the ruins of Ugarit are silent. You would never guess, in this green and peaceful setting, that there had once been a thriving seaport city here.

as well as a steady supply of students being trained. The work they had to do was also predictable. Every year, the harvest was collected and the state took its share of taxes. The scribes took charge of organizing and recording all of this. If their king conquered a new territory, they recorded the tribute that was paid to him. The work of a scribe varied very little from year to year.

In Ugarit, however, life was very different. Ships were coming and going every day. The port was full of foreign

DID YOU KNOW?

Two versions of the Ugarit alphabet have been identified: one has thirty different letters and was used for commercial purposes. Another, with just twenty-seven letters, seems to have been reserved only for religious uses.

seafarers and merchants, making deals and sending and receiving cargoes. The scribes who had to record all this buying, selling, and shipping would not necessarily have been working in their first language.

Sounding Things Out

Around 1400 BCE, therefore, they adopted what we would call an alphabet. This was not just a series of symbols, but also a set of characters, each of which corresponded to a sound. This allowed words to be written out quickly and easily. As long as you knew what the word sounded like, you could write it. It sounds obvious, but it was an intellectual revolution.

Even so, this alphabet was doomed to be forgotten. Another trading people, the Phoenicians, developed a different alphabet. The homeports of the Phoenicians were Tyre and Sidon, just a little way south along the

Mediterranean coast from Ugarit. Rather than adapting existing cuneiform characters, the Phoenicians created their alphabet from scratch. It seems to have been this one that formed the basis for the later Greek alphabet—and, so many centuries later, our own.

▶ Cuneiform continued to be used at Ugarit for more formal and prestigious texts. This inscription bears the seal of King Mursil II, which dates it to between 1345 and 1320 BCE.

A PERMANENT PEACE

IN 1274 BCE, THE EGYPTIAN AND HITTITE ARMIES FOUGHT EACH OTHER TO A STALEMATE AT THE BATTLE OF KADESH. FIFTEEN YEARS LATER, THEY SIGNED THE WORLD'S FIRST PEACE TREATY.

The city of Kadesh stood for centuries on the banks of the Orontes River in Syria. Around 1274 BCE there was a great battle there. An Egyptian army led by Pharaoh Ramses II had invaded the area. After several centuries during which Egypt had been on the defensive, the kingdom was feeling stronger. Ramses's father, Seti I, had started extending his empire into the Middle East in a series of victorious campaigns. Now Ramses himself was trying to continue his father's work of conquest.

But the Hittites had other ideas. From their homeland of Hatti, in the heart of Anatolia (modern Turkey), they had built an empire that extended south into Syria and Palestine, and east into the northern part of Mesopotamia. An important military power, the Hittites were not used to being beaten on the battlefield: they had no

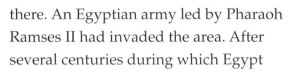
◄ The Hittites were among the most important military powers in the ancient Middle East. This stone carving of an archer was found at a site in modern Turkey.

THE TRANSLATION

The Treaty of Kadesh was the first formal and binding peace agreement that we know of. The Egyptians and Hittites also agreed that they would come to each other's assistance if either was attacked by a third party.

" Previously, from the beginning of time, the gods never allowed conflict to arise between Egypt's mighty ruler and the High Prince of Hatti. During the reign of my brother Muwatallis, High Prince of Hatti, though, there was war with Ramses Meri-Amon, great Pharaoh. But from this day on, Hattusilis, Great Prince of Hatti, is committed to making a lasting contract ... so that further fighting should forever be prevented.

Peace and brotherhood shall forever prevail between us... The children of the children of the Great Prince of Hatti will be at peace with the children of the children of Ramses Meri-Amon, great Pharaoh, for they too will live in brotherhood and peace. **"**

▲ The Egyptian copy of the treaty has been lost, but the Hittites' Akkadian version survives: a replica is displayed at the United Nations headquarters in New York.

Ramses had two temples carved out at Abu Simbel as a lasting monument to himself and his queen, Nefertari. However, the temples were relocated in the 1960s so they would not be submerged by the waters of the newly-built massive dam at Aswan.

intention of allowing the Egyptians to take their territories. The Hittites had been furious when Seti I had captured Kadesh a couple of years before, and

▼ Ramses II claimed to have won a glorious victory at the Battle of Kadesh. He had triumphant scenes displayed at his great temple at Abu Simbel.

had lost no time in recapturing it. They were not about to let go of it a second time.

Double Agents

But Ramses's men had captured two enemy soldiers. The prisoners told the pharaoh that the Hittites's main force was far away, near Aleppo. Ramses saw his chance, and pushed on toward the city as fast as his advance guard could go. This was risky, because it left his entire army stretched out over many miles in hostile country.

The pharaoh did not worry, though: even just with his vanguard, he had 20,000 infantry and more than two

thousand chariots. What he did not realize was that his two prisoners were agents of the Hittites. They had been sent out specially to fall into the Egyptians' hands as if by accident. They had then given their enemy an entirely misleading picture of the military situation. In fact, the Hittites were just nearby, standing at the ready almost 40,000 foot soldiers and three thousand chariots.

Muwatallis's heavy three-horse chariots led the charge, which left the Egyptian army reeling in shock and disbelief. The Egyptians were utterly defeated, their fighting spirit broken. Then, however, the triumphant Hittite soldiers stopped to plunder their defeated enemy, stripping the bodies of anything of value. They completely lost interest in the battle.

Holding his nerve, Ramses seized his chance to call his shattered forces back to order. Showing great courage and discipline, Ramses's forces returned to the attack and pushed the Hittites back.

Coming to Terms

Both sides claimed victory, though it could really only be described as an honorable draw. A balance of power resulted in the region. The two empires confirmed this when, fifteen years later, at Kadesh itself, they negotiated an "Eternal Treaty."

▶ Ramses II makes an impressive figure sitting on his throne. He was a brave and resourceful general—even if he did exaggerate his triumphs.

SARGON STATES HIS CASE

SARGON II WAS A GREAT CONQUERING KING, BUT HIS RISE TO POWER HAD BEEN CONTROVERSIAL. HE HAD APPEARED OUT OF NOWHERE TO SEIZE CONTROL IN ASSYRIA.

Suddenly, in 722 BCE, the people of Assyria discovered that they had a second king. A newcomer had been enthroned alongside Shalmaneser V. Some said he was Shalmaneser's younger brother, though nobody knew for sure. He may just have been some strong and ambitious official or soldier who had gained a hold over Shalmaneser. He called himself Sargon, and everyone would instantly have recognized the reference to Sargon the Great, the king who had built the Akkadian Empire almost a thousand years before.

A Doubtful Claim

The first Sargon had seized his throne by force. He gave himself the name Sargon because it meant "The Lawful King:" Though he knew his reign was not lawful, he hoped to persuade the Assyrian people otherwise.

► Attendants prepare a banquet for Sargon II. His origins may have been mysterious, but Sargon was destined to become one of Assyria's greatest kings.

WHAT DOES IT MEAN?

Sargon asks to be judged not by who he is—or who his ancestors were—but by what he has done in defense of Assyria, its empire, and its gods.

▲ Akkadian cuneiform is very concise, allowing for a lengthy text to be expressed in just a few lines. The first Mesopotamian scripts are believed to have been developed for keeping records of tax payments, trading transactions, and stored supplies.

66 These are my actions from the start of my reign to its fifteenth year: I crushed Khumbanigas, the King of Elam, on Kalu's plains. I took tribute from the Pharaoh of Egypt and from Samsie, Arabian Queen; It-amar of Sabea gave me gold, fragrant herbs, horses, and camels.

When Kiakku of Sinukhta blasphemed against the god Assur and refused to do him homage, I took him captive, along with thirty chariots and 7,350 soldiers... I set out to punish the unholy and insubordinate Chaldeans. Their King Merodach-Baladan heard my army was approaching, and fearing that his own cowardly army would crumble, he retreated, flying like an owl in the night, and took refuge in Ikbibel, Babylonia. He had all the idols brought from all the cities around, placing them all in the fortress of Dur-Iakin, whose walls he reinforced. Calling on the tribes of Gambul, Pukud, Tamun, Ruhua, and Khindar for their support, he dug in with them, preparing for a fight. He created a great ditch two thousand spans wide and ten feet deep in front of his wall. Then, digging channels to divert water from the Euphrates, filled it up to make his city an island ... I sent my warriors out in small bands along the canals and they conquered their enemies. The waters were colored red, like dyed wool, by the rebels' blood. 99

DID YOU KNOW?

Sargon made great contributions to Assyria. A ruler's achievements at this time were measured in conquests and tribute, and Sargon was immensely successful as a warrior general.

The Assyrians strongly suspected that this second Sargon was a usurper, but there was no stopping him. The death of Shalmaneser V that year does not seem to have been an assassination because he died on the battlefield. But it was certainly convenient for Sargon II, who swiftly had himself proclaimed Assyria's outright ruler.

This second Sargon had all the qualities of a king. No one could dispute that he was tough and resolute, even ruthless.

Doubts remained about who he really was, however, and about whether he actually had any right to be sitting on the throne.

Self-Advertisement

Sargon II, who reigned until his death in 705 BCE, also seems to have been uncomfortable with the question of his origins. He had his palaces decorated with inscriptions celebrating his own personal courage and his greatness as a king.

This sort of self-promotion was by no means unusual. Kings of the time were never slow to sing their own praises, but it is still striking that Sargon II's inscriptions dwell so much on his own personal qualities. Previous Assyrian kings had drawn attention to the glories of the ruling dynasties they belonged to, not just their own virtues.

▶ Sargon (right) gives his son Sennacherib the benefit of his fatherly advice. Sennacherib reigned after him, from 705 to 681 BCE.

◀ Sargon had a splendid new capital and palace-complex built in his own honor. The Dur-Sarrukin, which means Fortress of Sargon, is in Khorsabad, north of Mosul in Iraq.

SENNACHERIB GOES TO WAR

SARGON II'S SON SENNACHERIB WAS AS CONTROVERSIAL AS HIS FATHER, AND HIS OWN ACCOUNT OF HIS MOST FAMOUS CONQUEST IS DISPUTED TO THIS DAY.

The "Taylor Prism" is so-called after its discovery in 1830 by a certain Colonel Taylor, Britain's consul general in Baghdad. This hexagonal block, just over 5 inches (14 cm) in diameter and standing 15 inches (38 cm) tall, is inscribed all over its six faces.

The text tells us much of what we know about Sennacherib's military campaigns. But much remains in doubt. Sennacherib's most famous exploit was the Sack of Jerusalem in 701 BCE, when he captured and destroyed the ancestral capital of the Jews.

THE TRANSLATION

WHAT DOES IT MEAN?
Sennacherib stakes his claim to belong to the noble tradition of Assyrian conquering kings—despite a certain amount of evidence that his personal preference may have been for peace.

" Hezekiah, king of Judah, would not bow down to me. Forty-six of his key strongholds—great walled cities—as well as countless smaller towns in his territory were captured. My men brought siege-engines, razed them to the ground with battering-rams, attacked and took them by storm, stole in through breaches they had made in their walls or dug their way underneath them with mines and tunnels ... 200,150 people of high and low birth—both men and women—were taken captive. I carried countless horses, mules, asses, camels, cattle, and sheep.

The king himself took refuge in his royal city, caught like a bird in a cage. I built ramps and fortifications to stop people from leaving the city, trapping them inside in their misery...

The glory of my greatness overwhelmed Hezekiah. He was terrified. The Arabs and other mercenaries he had hired deserted him. Finally he had to submit to my authority and to pay me tribute: thirty talents of gold; eight hundred talents of

The Victory that Never Was?

Yet the Jewish scribes insisted this event never happened. Their version of events can be read in the Bible, in the Second Book of Kings, chapters 18 to 19. They admit that the Assyrian king did succeed in conquering most of Hezekiah's kingdom of Judah. But the capital was saved, they say. The angel of the Lord came down

silver; gems ... couches and chairs inlaid with ivory; elephant hides and tusks; ebony, boxwood and other rich treasures, along with his daughters, his wives, his musicians—men and women... All these things I had brought to me in Nineveh. **"**

▶ Taylor's Prism—a fired ceramic form, which was inscribed with the story of Sennacherib's great deeds, was found in 1830 among the ruins of the king's capital at Nineveh.

during the night and killed the Assyrians' foremost warriors. Just when victory seemed assured, Sennacherib was forced to retreat. Returning home, he was assassinated by his own sons. The Second Book of Chronicles confirms this story.

▲ Apparently an unwilling war-maker, Sennacherib was forced by unrest to invade Babylonia, Egypt, and Judah, homeland of the Jews.

▶ On the east bank of the Tigris—across the river from the modern city of Mosul, in northern Iraq— Sennacherib created a splendid new Assyrian capital at Nineveh.

Constructive Conqueror

We cannot know the truth of such stories, although in some ways it hardly matters: Sennacherib seems to have been more interested in building cities than in destroying them. He devoted much of his life to rebuilding Assyria's old capital at Nineveh. He probably set up this new center for himself to put distance between his own reign and that of his father. (Sargon II, who barely gets a mention in Sennacherib's inscriptions.) But Sennacherib clearly had a creative vision that he wanted to express along with his military exploits.

DID YOU KNOW?

Sennacherib's invasion of Egypt came to an equally unfortunate end, according to the later Greek historian Herodotus (c.484–c.425 BCE). His army had conquered the entire kingdom and Sennacherib was on the point of taking the pharaoh's capital. However, that night, while his army slept, thousands of field mice stole into the soldiers' tents. The mice chewed up the soldiers' bowstrings and the straps of their shields, so they could not fight.

THE FIRST FLOOD

HUNDREDS OF YEARS BEFORE THE BIBLICAL STORY OF NOAH WAS WRITTEN DOWN, A SUMERIAN POEM TOLD OF A CATACLYSMIC FLOOD THAT COVERED THE ENTIRE EARTH.

The Epic of Gilgamesh is believed to be the world's first work of literature. It was written down in Sumeria in the second half of the third millennium BCE. As with other early works of literature, it seems likely that, by that time, it had already been circulating by oral tradition for generations, perhaps even centuries.

An Unusual Hero

An epic poem, the work describes the heroic deeds of the great Gilgamesh, an early king of Uruk, who reigned around 2600 BCE. No ordinary man—not even an

▼ Gilgamesh was born here in Uruk about 4,600 years ago. There is no hint now that these ruins were once a bustling city, or that this parched landscape was ever flooded.

THE TRANSLATION

WHAT DOES IT MEAN?

The account of the flood in the Epic of Gilgamesh is not just a marvelous story and a powerful piece of literature in its own right. It also points to parallels and possible connections between some of the world's first civilizations.

66 The angry gods felt in their hearts the urge to send a mighty flood … All day, the wind blew from the south; fast and strong it came, plunging the mountain deep in water; the waves advanced like an army, crashing over the people … The gods themselves were terrified at what they had done: they retreated to Anu's heaven where they huddled, cowering together like frightened dogs. Ishtar's screams were like those of a woman giving birth: her voice, usually so soft and gentle, screeched …

"How could I have called for a catastrophe to destroy my people? I have only just given birth to my people and the world becomes an ocean, and they like fish! " **99**

▶ Written in Akkadian cuneiform, this fragment of the Epic of Gilgamesh was one of a series discovered in the ruins of the Royal Library at Nineveh in 1849.

45

DID YOU KNOW?

The version of the Epic of Gilgamesh we know today is a relatively late one. The Assyrian scribes of King Ashurbanipal wrote it down on a series of clay tablets. Ashurbanipal, who reigned from 668–627 BCE, put the tablets in his Royal Library at Nineveh.

▼ Created in Hittite Syria around 1000 BCE, this stone carving shows the hero Gilgamesh flanked by demigods who hold a winged sun—symbol of royal power—above his head.

ordinary king—he was believed to have been the son of a goddess.

Actually, Gilgamesh is no ordinary hero either. As his story starts, he is no better than a bully. Far from protecting his people, he oppresses them. They pray to the earth-goddess Shamhat for help, and she sends a wild man, Enkidu. He has a series of fights with Gilgamesh. Over time, though, Enkidu and Gilgamesh come to respect each other and finally they become friends. Gilgamesh even persuades his mother to adopt Enkidu so that they will be brothers. Under Enkidu's influence, Gilgamesh changes his ways, growing

into a kind and considerate person and a responsible king.

Then the wild man, Enkidu, dies and Gilgamesh is overcome with shock and grief. He is also shaken because he has never thought about death until now. According to the epic, he goes off on a quest to find the secret of everlasting life. On his way he meets a couple: Utnapishtim and his wife. They are the only human survivors of a terrible flood sent by Anu (god of the heavens) and Ishtar (goddess of fertility and love) to drown the earth because the gods are enraged by the ingratitude of humans.

Flood Legends

The parallels between Utnapishtim and Noah are obvious: Utnapishtim even builds himself an ark, under the direction of the sun god Shamash. The writers of the Old Testament scripture may not have been aware of the Epic of Gilgamesh, but the similarities seem too close to have been a complete coincidence.

Experts believe that there was probably a common stock of traditional stories that all Middle Eastern peoples shared, including the Sumerians and the early Jews who wrote the Bible. In fact, flood legends existed in other ancient cultures, such as the myths of Greece and those of India.

▶ Gilgamesh holds the ferocious lion he has captured as though it were nothing more than a domestic cat in this sculpture from Sargon II's palace at Khorsabad.

BABYLON REBUILT

IN 689 BCE, SENNACHERIB'S ASSYRIAN ARMY HAD LEFT BABYLON A SMOKING RUIN. IN THE 670S BCE, HIS SON ESARHADDON REBUILT THE CITY AND ITS FAMOUS TEMPLE OF MARDUK AT ESAGILA.

Sennacherib's sacking of Babylon had left his own kingdom very badly damaged. Assyria had won the war but lost its reputation. Babylon was special, seen by many across Mesopotamia as the center of the world. Most people regarded its destruction as an act of sacrilege. And the temple of Marduk, the city's supreme deity, was famous far and wide. What sort of savages could have burned it down?

The Official Version
Esarhaddon's proclamations turned everything upside-down. Babylon had been destroyed by the order of the gods, he claimed. It had been because of the wickedness of the Babylonians that this terrible, divine punishment had come down upon them. (Esarhaddon does not even mention any role his father might have played.)

▶ Sennacherib sits back and watches his forces get to work on Babylon's defenses. The sacking of the city in 689 BCE was to have consequences that would last a very long time.

THE TRANSLATION

WHAT DOES IT MEAN?

Esarhaddon's inscription is a superb example of what in modern-times we call political "spin." He presents Assyria's war crimes as interventions of the gods and portrays himself as the spiritual savior of the Babylonian people.

66 Great king, mighty monarch, lord of all, king of the land of Assur, ruler of Babylon, faithful shepherd, beloved of Marduk, lord of lords...

Once during a previous ruler's reign there were bad omens. The city insulted its gods and was destroyed at their command. They chose me, Esarhaddon, to restore everything to its rightful place, to calm their anger, and soothe their rage.

You, Marduk, gave the land of Assur to me to look after. The Gods of Babylon meanwhile told me to rebuild their shrines and see that proper religious observances were being carried out in their palace, Esagila.... I called up my laborers and conscripted all the people of Babylonia. I set them to work digging up the ground and carrying the earth away in baskets. 99

◄ Carved into a baked clay prism, Esarhaddon's account of Esagila's restoration was placed in the foundations of the rebuilt shrine.

All of a sudden, we are asked to see the Assyrians not as violent destroyers, but as peacemakers and rebuilders. How fortunate the Babylonians are to have a conqueror like Esarhaddon! Who else would have been prepared to go to so much trouble to restore the Babylonians' relationship with the gods that they have so badly alienated? No effort is too great for the Assyrian king, it seems. At a groundbreaking ceremony for the new Esagila, Esarhaddon personally digs the first spade full of soil. "To instill respect and fear for the power of Marduk in the people," his inscription claims, "I myself picked up the first basket of earth, raised it on to my head and carried it..."

A Disputed Memory

Ironically, in modern times Western tradition has taken the side of the Assyrian conquerors regarding this controversial event. This is because Christianity and the Bible have influenced so many Western attitudes toward events of the time. The Jewish scribes who wrote the Old Testament were bitterly against Babylon, and all it stood for. They could never forget that their people were taken captive by the Babylonians, even though it had happened a century after Sennacherib's destruction of the Esagila.

In 586 BCE, Babylonian King Nebuchadnezzar II had put down a rebellion among his Jewish subjects. He then carried off their community leaders and priests and kept them in Babylon, in forced exile. That way, he prevented them from organizing more resistance to his rule. It was not until the Persians conquered Babylon in 537 BCE that the Jews were allowed to return. The Persian Emperor Cyrus the Great was an enlightened and generous ruler: he even rebuilt the Temple of Jerusalem, which Nebuchadnezzar's men had demolished.

Even so, the bitter memory of Babylon stayed with the Jews for centuries. They took it for granted that Sennacherib's sacking had been a just punishment for a wicked city.

▼ Marduk, father of the gods, was the supreme deity of the Babylonians and their city's great protector. He was often represented in the form of a bull, as in this carving.

THE WORLD THROUGH BABYLONIAN EYES

THIS MAP SHOWS US THE WORLD AS THE SUMERIANS SAW IT, WITH THEIR CAPITAL CITY RIGHT AT THE CENTER. STUDYING THIS MAP MAY HELP US TO UNDERSTAND THE MESOPOTAMIAN MIND.

The tablet dates from about 600 BCE—a very late point in the history of the ancient Mesopotamian civilizations. By this time, the cultures of Greece and Rome were already on the rise in southern Europe. But if the peoples of Sumeria were concerned that the high point of their greatness might be

THE INSCRIPTION

The earth—or at least its land area—is shown as being circular. It is not shaped like a sphere, as we would see it, but a round, flat disk. Living between two great rivers, the Mesopotamians seem to have had only the haziest idea of what the sea might be.

WHAT DOES IT MEAN?
Any map tells us as much about the mind that made it as about the country it represents. This one reflects the supreme self-confidence of a Sumeria with Babylon at its center.

Here, while it is depicted as surrounding the earth completely, it is described as just another river, though a river of "bitter" water. This was presumably a reference to its saltiness. The ocean here is shown as marking the end of the world. There is no hint that it might open up ways to other countries. The people who made this map were definitely not seafarers.

Just above the center of the map, the city of Babylon is shown as a rectangle. It straddles the straight lines that represent the Euphrates River. Parallel lines near the bottom seem to represent the marshes at the southern end of Mesopotamia. Further out, around the edge of the land area, are seven small circles. These represent key cities. The cuneiform inscription names the neighboring kingdoms Armenia (to the west) and Elam (to the east), as well as a number of cities, including Assur, the Assyrian capital.

▲ It may seem amusing to us to see the world presented so small with a now-forgotten city at its center, but in seventh-century BCE Sumeria, this must have been the way that things appeared to the people living then.

DID YOU KNOW?

Archaeologists found the tablet of baked clay during excavations at Sippar, now known as Tell Abu Habbah, 22 miles (35 km) southwest of Baghdad, Iraq.

passing, this world map gives us no hint of that.

To begin with, it hardly gives us any hint of anything at all. It seems just a jumble of assorted shapes and crisscross scrawls. Only when we look at it more closely do we see a clear form beginning to emerge. The map does not follow the natural contours of the landscape, or the courses of rivers in the way a modern map would. Instead, it shows the way the

world was organized in the Mesopotamian mind. Old Babylon, a great power during the second millennium BCE, had gone into decline after that time, and its capital and territories had become possessions of Assyria.

Babylon and Beyond

But then the seventh century BCE had brought the rise of a Neo-Babylonian Empire, restoring the city to its former status. It must have been very satisfying for the Babylonian mapmaker to be able to show their own city as the center of the world, and to put Assur in its place at the earth's outermost margins.

It is not strictly true that the Babylonian mapmakers show nothing beyond the sea. There are groups of triangles on the map that look like the points of the compass at first glance, but the mapmakers appear to have intended them to represent islands.

Just what kind of islands were they meant to be? They could possibly be landmasses. But if so, it is hard to guess which countries they might be. One, we are told, is the land of light more bright than any star; another is a place of darkness, where the sun is hidden and nothing can be seen. These might have been real, geographical lands, but it seems more likely that the triangles were meant to represent spiritual places, early versions of what we might call heaven or hell.

▲ Babylon became a great power during the reign of King Nebuchadnezzar II (605–562 BCE). Here he receives the submission of King Jeconiah of Judah, in 597 BCE.

▼ Ancient Babylon was for centuries seen as the ultimate city—and not only by the Babylonians.

NEBUCHADNEZZAR'S BOAST

THE BOASTS OF AN ANCIENT EMPIRE-BUILDER STRUCK A CHORD WITH
MODERN CONQUERORS. BRITISH COLONISTS TOOK THIS ARROGANT
INSCRIPTION BACK TO DISPLAY IN LONDON.

By the end of the eighteenth century, British imperial power was on the rise. The country was already establishing a presence in India and the Middle East. As yet, Britain's government was not officially involved: a private firm, the East India Company, organized the conquest of new territories and trade with native peoples. Iraq was still under the rule of the Turkish Ottoman Empire.

But Ottoman power had been in decline for decades, and the company was on the lookout for opportunities wherever they occurred, so it made sure it had a representative there. This representative was Sir Harford Jones Brydges (1764–1847). Like any educated gentleman of his time, he was aware of recent advances in what we now call archaeology.

◄ Characterized as a villain in the Bible, Nebuchadnezzar II loomed large in much later Christian tradition. Here he features in a medieval woodcarving.

THE TRANSLATION

▼ Over 2,000 years after its creation, the claims of the "East India House" inscription inspired the British who were at that time beginning to build an empire of their own.

66 Nebuchadnezzar, king of Babylon, famous monarch, worshiper of Marduk, honorer of the great Nebu, god of wisdom ... I am the valiant son of Nabopolassar, king of Babylon ... I extended the walls of Babylon all the way around the city. I had a deep defensive ditch dug and used the earth to create massive ramparts.... On one side I placed a tower as tall as a mountain. Great gates of pinewood, armored with copper plate, kept the enemy out of my unvanquished city. I brought deep waters to make a moat as wide as any sea ... I fortified these defenses and fitted Babylon out to be a city of treasures. 99

At this time, the crucial contribution of Mesopotamia was gradually being uncovered in excavations. So Brydges was naturally interested when he heard a large and elaborately inscribed basalt slab had been unearthed in the ruins of Babylon.

Pride and Punishment

He grew especially interested when the inscription turned out to have been created in the name of Nebuchadnezzar—a name familiar to Christians from the Bible. There, in the Book of Daniel (chapter 4, verse 33), the king of Babylon is punished for his arrogance. He is driven out into the fields, where he is forced "to eat grass like oxen … until his hair was grown like eagle's feathers and his nails like bird's claws."

Had Nebuchadnezzar's pride really brought on so shocking a fall? All the evidence is that this was wishful thinking on the part of the Jewish scribes. They had no reason to love the king who in 586 BCE had not only destroyed Jerusalem but also abducted the leaders of their community, taking them back to his capital for the fifty-year "Babylonian Captivity."

◀ The modern artist can only guess at what the famous "Hanging Gardens of Babylon" were like—if they even existed at all. The traditional story is that Nebuchadnezzar built them for his queen, Amytis.

In reality, Nebuchadnezzar's power was unchallenged. His Babylonian Empire was the greatest power of the age. And Babylon itself was the greatest city of the era: visitors from far and wide wondered at its spectacular walls and gates, and everyone who saw them marveled at its glorious palaces and fine temples.

▲ Babylon's Ishtar Gate was sacred to the Mesopotamian goddess of love, fertility, and war. It was excavated in 1902 by German archaeologists. This accurate reconstruction is in Berlin, Germany.

From Babylon to Britain

Sir Harford Brydges and his countrymen were naturally curious about this relic of a king who they had all read about at Sunday school, but they were also inspired by his imperialist example. What Babylon had been, in the very earliest centuries of civilization, they wanted Britain to be in the modern age. It seemed fitting that this inscription should be shipped back to London and displayed at the company's headquarters, East India House. Now the British Empire has gone the same way as that of Babylon, but Nebuchadnezzar's inscription can still be seen in London to this day.

GLOSSARY

archaeology—The study of past civilizations through the traces they left behind, such as remains of buildings, pottery, weaponry, and tombs.

barbarian—Someone who (in the opinion of the speaker) is uncivilized. The word is said to come from the Greek and Roman view that the peoples they conquered talked a nonsense-language that sounded, to their ears, like "Ba-ba-ba."

barbarism—Barbarism is being barbaric, or doing the kind of thing a barbarian would do.

blaspheme—Say something insulting about God or the gods.

ceramic—Made of pottery.

cataclysmic—A massive and often violent event that involves huge destruction and upheaval, bringing great changes.

conspirators—A group who plot against another group or person, often to gain political power or influence.

demigod—Literally "half-god." Nowadays generally used for a person we think is marvelous in some way, but some ancient religions did believe in beings that were half-man, half-god.

dynasty—A family of rulers who pass on power from one generation to the next.

empire—The wider area outside its own borders over which a powerful state may rule. Assur itself was geographically small, for example. At various times, though, it ruled over much of Mesopotamia.

epic—A long story, often told in the form of a poem, about great heroes and their adventures. Often an epic tells the mythical story of how a particular civilization started.

imperial—Relating to or associated with an empire.

incantation—A chant, which is often repetitive, used in prayer or in casting magic spells.

medieval—From the Latin *medium* ("middle") and *aevum* ("age"): the period in European history between the time of the Greeks and Romans and the

Renaissance ("rebirth") of Western Europe. It is often also called the "Middle Ages."

mortal—Literally, anything that dies. In ancient mythology the term is often used for living men and women. That way they are distinguished from "immortals"—those gods and spirits that will live forever.

omen—A sign indicating good or bad fortune to come.

oral—Traditional stories, songs, poems, or knowledge that is handed down from generation to generation by word of mouth, rather than in written form.

quest—A journey in search of some special goal, often undertaken by a mythical hero.

sacrilege—Some behavior or action that offends God or the gods. It differs from blasphemy in that it is an action, rather than something that is said.

scribe—Someone whose profession it is to write. In ancient civilizations the majority of people would have been unable to read or write, so the scribes held an important position in society.

shrine—Any place or building that is holy.

tribute—A sort of tax, paid by people to the king or state that has conquered them.

tyranny—A government or ruler that holds complete power and oppresses all opposition.

usurp—To take a position that belongs, by rights, to someone else. A "usurper" might bring down a king and take his throne for himself.

TIMELINE OF MESOPOTAMIA

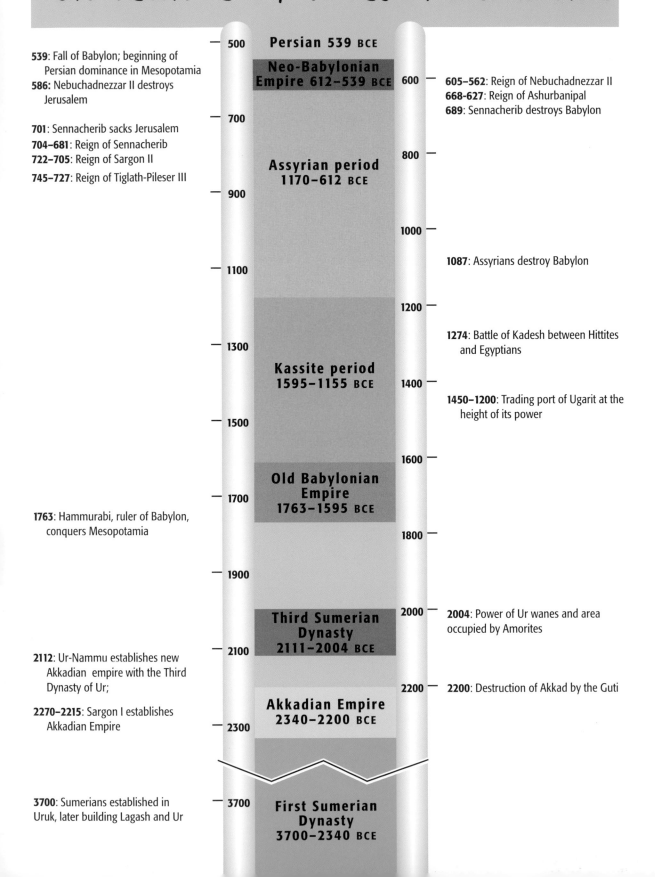

539: Fall of Babylon; beginning of Persian dominance in Mesopotamia

586: Nebuchadnezzar II destroys Jerusalem

701: Sennacherib sacks Jerusalem

704–681: Reign of Sennacherib

722–705: Reign of Sargon II

745–727: Reign of Tiglath-Pileser III

1763: Hammurabi, ruler of Babylon, conquers Mesopotamia

2112: Ur-Nammu establishes new Akkadian empire with the Third Dynasty of Ur;

2270–2215: Sargon I establishes Akkadian Empire

3700: Sumerians established in Uruk, later building Lagash and Ur

Persian 539 BCE

Neo-Babylonian Empire 612–539 BCE

Assyrian period 1170–612 BCE

Kassite period 1595–1155 BCE

Old Babylonian Empire 1763–1595 BCE

Third Sumerian Dynasty 2111–2004 BCE

Akkadian Empire 2340–2200 BCE

First Sumerian Dynasty 3700–2340 BCE

500
600
700
800
900
1000
1100
1200
1300
1400
1500
1600
1700
1800
1900
2000
2100
2200
2300
3700

605–562: Reign of Nebuchadnezzar II

668-627: Reign of Ashurbanipal

689: Sennacherib destroys Babylon

1087: Assyrians destroy Babylon

1274: Battle of Kadesh between Hittites and Egyptians

1450–1200: Trading port of Ugarit at the height of its power

2004: Power of Ur wanes and area occupied by Amorites

2200: Destruction of Akkad by the Guti

FURTHER INFORMATION

Books

Mehta-Jones, Shilpa. *Life in Ancient Mesopotamia* (Peoples of the Ancient World). New York: Crabtree Publishing, 2004.

Quigley, Mary and Jane Shuter. *Mesopotamia* (Excavating the Past). Minneapolis, MN: Heinemann, 2006.

Schomp, Virginia. *The Ancient Mesopotamians* (Myths of the World). New York: Marshall Cavendish, 2009.

Steele, Philip and John Farndon. *Mesopotamia* (DK Eyewitness). New York: DK Children, 2007.

Websites

Ancient Mesopotamia for Kids—www.mesopotamia.mrdonn.org/

The British Museum: Mesopotamia—www.mesopotamia.co.uk/menu.html

Gateways to Babylon—www.gatewaystobabylon.com

Kids Konnect: Ancient Mesopotamia—www.kidskonnect.com/content/view/257/27/

THE AUTHOR

Michael Kerrigan has written dozens of books for children and young adults over the last twenty years. He is the author of *The Ancients in Their Own Words* (2008), *A Dark History: The Roman Emperors* (2008), and *Ancient Greece and the Mediterranean* (part of the BBC Ancient Civilizations series). He also works as a columnist, book reviewer, and feature writer for publications including the *Scotsman* and the *Times Literary Supplement*. He lives in Edinburgh, Scotland.

INDEX